Ron Gooden

The Infallible Truth

Ron Gooden

The Infallible Truth

Truly Immutable

Blessed Hope Publishing

Imprint

Cover image: www.ingimage.com

Publisher:
Blessed Hope Publishing
is a trademark of
International Book Market Service Ltd., member of OmniScriptum Publishing Group
17 Meldrum Street, Beau Bassin 71504, Mauritius

Printed at: see last page
ISBN: 978-613-7-83690-3

Table of Contents

Introduction

The infallible Truth is the Love of GOD above all that is negative. It is the realm of Divine standard; the upright meditation of those who seek the higher rather than the lower. Nothing can penetrate the realm of eternity but the infallible Truth. All that is associated with goodness and positivity is found in the infallible Truth. It is the association with infinity, the heights of Holiness, and the depths of the true transcendence of all things.

The infallible Truth explores all the ins and outs of infallibility. From the infallible mindset, to the exploration of all that is enduring, the infallible Truth delves into the hard facts that can only be confirmed by the harmony of life and being. Positive thinking has its foundation in the infallible Truth, and all that has been taught about of the law of attraction can be seen in extreme positivity through its lens.

To think, speak, believe, feel and do in the highest according to the standard of Divinity is the integrity of the infallible Truth. To let go of all that hinders and hold onto all that brings progression in every sphere of living is the infallible Truth beyond measure. All those who seek to improve circumstances of every kind must first seek to improve the mind and heart. And in this the infallible Truth will bear good fruit for all those who seek freedom. True liberation can only be attained through rigorous struggle to attain perfection in the very highest. And those who seek to be liberated outside of this can never know the MASTER.

Liberate yourself first in thought. Then you can liberate every outlet of the innate Potential that lies dormant in spiritual blindness. There are many anchors in which one can direct his/her point of focus to come into the heights of Truth. However, the infallible Truth seeks to cover all the bases that hinders, as well as the foundation and pinnacle of all that brings true progress in every facet of existence.

Chapter One

Selfishness

The majority of the human population has descended into the detriment of selfishness, a vice that causes us all to be cold, distant, and unkind. However, most do not know of the downfall of selfishness as they do not understand its very nature; the nature which is of evil that promotes inconsideration towards others, and puts self-consideration before all things and people, even before GOD. This has been brought to the very extent where no one sees or hears anyone but their own selfishness.

It is only when we abide in the neglect of selfishness can we see the detriment of selfishness in its full scope. And only when we give into selflessness can we enter the realm that sees selfishness as a wicked trait that disregards others for the sake of self-assertion. One must look beyond the world of mortality and put selfishness into the perspective of Truth in order to overcome its sway on the soul.

Anything that has to do with self will surely put us under the darkness of inconsideration towards others. We must first look above and beyond self-seeking in order to live in harmony with the great purpose of Love. And in so doing we will find our own purpose wrapped up in Love and selflessness that speaks to the heart of the potential Saint within. Only when we live for others instead of for self will we find our true impersonal being that lives for and enables others to be their best. Then can we say that we are enablers of Love; sustainers of righteousness; and preservers of all that is good. Only at this juncture in our journey will we find true fulfillment and joy everlasting. This is the true purpose of man, and only if we embrace it with all that we are will we live up to our full potential.

Many since the beginning of time have sought to please themselves and no one else. But only when we let go of selfish behavior will we find indescribable pleasure that goes beyond all mortality; beyond the suffering of emptiness; beyond the hindrance of self-seeking; and beyond the scope of all that is wrapped up in the primal existence of man.

Never should we put ourselves before others, but we should give ourselves unto selfless Love, for only then will we lift our souls beyond carelessness, inconsideration, and selfishness that destroy and corrupt hearts and minds. Nothing will ever be greater than selfless Love, for in Love lies all power, wisdom, understanding, and Truth. Selfishness seeks to steal away these things from our very grip, but only when we live in the light of this and act accordingly will selfishness be utterly eradicated.

Nothing good can strive in the heart of those who are selfish. Selfishness must first be cast out before anything good can dwell in the heart of any man. Think not that you must compete and fight for your provisions, for therein lies the foolishness of selfishness. Instead, give yourself wholly to selflessness, and the selfless nature shall find the true provision of all things, in and through kindness.

There is never any true justification for selfishness, not even if others are selfish towards you. For selfishness cannot cast out selfishness, it must be cast out only by that which is on the opposite pole. Selfishness begets selfishness, but Love and selflessness begets Love and selflessness. The conclusion of selfishness is that it has no part to play in goodness or progress, but its opposite which is selflessness in Love, will bear good fruit for the sustenance of both giver and receiver. This is infallible Truth.

Chapter Two

Carnality

The carnality of man is his downfall. All throughout the world we can see carnality playing the largest role in and throughout society. Man has turned to carnality because he has forgotten to live in the SPIRIT of GOD, instead of his senses. Therefore, he lives strictly to gratify his senses. When this is so, we find ourselves paying attention to the heard, instead of the unheard; the seen, instead of the unseen; the carnal, instead of the Divine; and the mortal, instead of the immortal.

The fact is that, unless we search out the perfect; ask of the sacred; and knock on the door of that which is eternal; we will never find that which is true. Instead, we shall only find that which is temporary, and that which is false.

When we neglect these Truths, then we become carnal, looking at only what the carnal eyes can see; never seeing that which is beyond the physical plane. It is when we fix our utmost attention on the things of the physical world, do we lose sight of the realm that is Divine. Only when we seek for fulfillment and satisfaction beyond the world of the carnal can we remember that there is a spiritual realm of Truth to be found within. It is then that we shall know that there is a level of consciousness beyond the external stimuli of the world that far surpasses all mortality. Only then can we know how to treasure, and hone how much we breath the heavenly atmosphere; and how to know the beginning of infallibility, and the end of infinity.

These are the inestimable and priceless gifts we forfeit when we focus only on the delusions of the carnal world. Those who store up their riches in heaven instead of the earth will find that true enlightenment is a much more valuable gift than vanity and carnal pleasure. We must cease from all carnal desire and wish only to please the MASTER of masters. Then and only then can we know the unlimited expression and Love of the HOLY ONE. It is only at this point can we truly harness our latent powers, and awaken our dormant potential.

Many talk about how they think heaven is so great, and it is the wish of everyone to go to heaven and see all their friends and relatives when they get there. But they all forget the discipline and patience required to be fortified in the wisdom of heaven. Such discipline can only be acquired by untiring dedication, and the pinnacle of ceaseless effort, coupled with sincerity and eagerness that outweighs every other yearning and longing. And this is why not many can confirm CHRIST in HIS words when HE said **"heaven is within you"**. In the space of the mind we are supposed to be able to hear all the Divine, including the CREATOR of all in harmony. We are to know immediately when something is wrong, and penetrate all Truth with precision and intricacy. Instead we only think we know things, instead of being sure, only seeing the delusion and effect of all causes, instead of the causes themselves, and are trapped wholly by the carnal senses and traits.

It is only at the end of this agonizing entrapment; the imprisonment of the physical senses, will we begin to ask the most important questions. Questions such as, what is my purpose? What path am I to take? By this time, the soul has been overwhelmed by strife, and asks these questions in desperation after years of wandering in the wilderness of gratification.

LOVE of HOLINESS, wisdom, GOD, and all that is good can in no way be honored or enjoyed when carnality is at play. This is the infallible Truth regarding carnality.

Chapter Three

Ego

Ego has been the downfall of many since the beginning of time. Ego is the opinionated man; the man that always has opinions in which he can in no way prove are true. It is the intellectual side of man that thinks he knows all, yet knows nothing. But furthermore, ego is the self that always wants to be right, to win, and to prove himself that he is right and deserves to win.

We must first understand that only when the inner voice of discernment is silenced by cooperation can we experience the stillness and silence of Truth. Then we will know that the ego is never right as it always tries to defend itself for the sake of being right. However, no one can be right or know that they are right at any time without the confirmation of stillness that goes far beyond the mind-chatter and confusion of ego.

The fact is that if we feel discomfort because of the opinions of others, as well as constant affliction from their opinions because their opinions go against ours; then we are not free from the torment of ego. As long as we have opinions that are not confirmed by silence and stillness within, then we are not set free from the ego. Ego feels the need to have supremacy over others in regards to opinion and having its own way according to its own sentiments. And unless we are set free from such ego we cannot experience the bliss of silent and still confirmation within that in no way, shape, or form feels the need to have supremacy over others.

Ego is always competitive in the need to feel right. But only the confirmation of stillness and silence is truly immutable. Only when we admit that being right has nothing to do with supremacy over others, but is supremacy over self towards the end of true freedom, can we be liberated by the light. Infallibility is attainable by man, but only when we let go of the need of supremacy by means of the ego can we truly be infallible and immutable in the highest, without feeling the need to prove that we are right and that others are wrong.

Opinion has always confused and tormented man to the point that he has beliefs that he cannot prove, but yet sticks by them, simply because of the ego which is detached from the liberation of Truth. Only when we let go of opinion, and by extension ego, which is the need to feel right all the time at the cost of Truth, can we truly be liberated. When we guard an opinion we simply give up the search for Truth and cling to the ego which leans to illusions that seemingly confirms our own biases.

Opinion and bias are one in the same; and only when we let go of opinion can we overcome bias within our own hearts. We must not form opinions, but we must always yearn for Truth, even if it goes against us in every way, shape, and form. The fact is that we have all formed opinions because of external stimuli, and only by looking inward for the Truth can we truly come out of the delusion of opinion and ego. When we have learned this we need to let go of all that we think is Truth and light in search of immutable and infallible Truth that cannot be disputed. Only then can we find the Truth within and be at one with it. Otherwise, we would only assume because of the bias that we are inclined to, and ultimately lose sight of the Truth in obscurity.

We must first let go of all opinions and the feeling of the need to always be right over everything and everyone else. Only then can we take the first step towards the sincere search for Truth above all opinion and ego. It is only then will we know that what is correct and true has nothing to do with opinion or ego, but has everything to do with infallible Truth.

Chapter Four

Sorrow

Sorrow has strangled the joy and happiness out of many. Almost everyone feels sorrow at one or more points in their lives. Sorrow is the feeling and thought of being wronged or disappointed. It is a deep feeling of distress caused by loss, disappointment, or other misfortune suffered personally or for others. However, no matter what loss, disappointment, or misfortune we suffer; it is never a valid reason to be sorrowful.

Only when we learn that all things happen for a reason no matter how unfortunate they might seem will we learn to embrace all that happens to, for, by and in us. Sorrow stems from some form of regret, and only when we learn that we are never to regret anything, can we truly embrace the present moment and live up to our true potential. No matter what might seem to have gone wrong we are to embrace all things in our lives as lessons on the journey of refinement. In order for us to come to full maturity in every aspect of our being, we must embrace all that happens as lessons for us to elevate, do better, and take the next step on our journey in life.

Whether it be the death of a loved one, and unrealized dream, failure, or anything else; we are to embrace it as stepping stones for us to reach the next level of our life's journey. Never should circumstances bring us sorrow. Instead they should encourage us to walk the path that is set before us, and not turn to the right or the left. Take for example the loss of a loved one. We should take it as a necessity in the cycle of life, and that it happened for a reason. When misfortune afflicts us, we should see it as a sign to steer ourselves in the right direction.

We must testify that misfortune only happens when we are on the wrong track in order to correct our way of life and our decisions. And many things that we feel we should be sorrowful over should be seen as necessary. Therefore, we should see all things as necessary and not live in sorrow or regret. Instead we should embrace all that happens as a means to steer us on the right path.

Sorrow comes with a certain perspective. The perspective that says this or that should not have happened and it is something to be sorrowful or regretful about. But when we change our perspective and think that everything happens for the benefit of our own good, then we can embrace all that happens in our lives, instead of being sorrowful and regretful. What we see as misfortune should be embraced as necessary for us to advance and take the next step in life on the journey of fulfillment. Otherwise, we will not advance in life, but remain stagnant and regress.

It is only when we accept all circumstances as necessary to help us to do better and to advance in life can we overcome sorrow, and see it as a delusion of conception, and an illusion of perspective. Only when we conceive that something is to be sorrowful over do we begin to perceive sorrow in our lives. Instead, conceive that all things whether they seem like misfortunes or not are meant to teach us a lesson and help us advance to the next step on our life's journey. Then we will perceive all things as stepping stones on the journey of life, and wholly cast out sorrow in all aspects of our lives.

Sorrow will never help us advance, but will keep us stagnant until we regress or overcome its snare. Sorrow is a mere delusion that must be cast out of the conception. This is infallible Truth.

Chapter Five

Hardship

Hardship has been with mankind since the beginning of time. However, only very few understand the very nature of hardship. Many ask, why me? The majority feel as if they deserve better than the hardship they have been dealt. But this is only because they do not know why they face hardship. Most believe that it is just random that they have a hard time in life. Some even believe that it is the attack of supernatural forces such as the devil. All of which are delusions of the mind.

We must first of all know that hardship does not come from any external force, but is the reflection of the inward state. Only when we go outside of the realm of LOVE do we experience hardship. This is because LOVE is the governing power above all powers, the governing law above all laws. And only when we understand this along with the very nature of LOVE do we come to the unravelling of all hardship.

The origin of hardship is from the inward state of rebellion against the path that is laid out before us. Only when we stray from this path do we begin to experience hardship. And man by experiencing hardship must see it as a portent that he needs to get back on the track of his life's path. The GOD of creation does not bring us hardship, but it is the very result of rebellion against the path that He has laid out before us.

The nature of hardship is meant to teach and bring to our attention the fact that we have fallen away from the Divine path laid out before us by the CREATOR of the worlds. Hardship must be seen by man as the result of going astray. It must be seen as a portent that we are taking the wrong path and the wrong approach in life. Only then will we know the purpose of hardship and learn how to cooperate with its warning to get back on the Divine path that is laid out for us. We co-operate with hardship by changing our course and approach in whatever area of life we are facing hardship. And only by searching inward and listening to the voice of conscience can we figure out where we have gone wrong and what needs to change.

We must learn that life was never meant to be hard. And by looking at those areas of life that brings hardship we can see where, why, and how we have gone wrong. And by this we find the root and remedy of all hardship. We then need to co-operate best with all that will avert hardship at every point. By bringing in harmony the elements that will avert hardship, we overcome and become masters of our life's experience.

It is at this juncture that we will see the point and purpose of all hardship. It is meant to teach a lesson; for us to trace back our steps to the point where things have gone wrong and correct it by proper thought and action. Hardship is meant to bring about conscious reflection of all that we think, say, feel, and do. And by reflecting we can trace hardship to our wrongful thoughts, words, emotions, and deeds. Only wrong thoughts, words, emotions, and deeds will bring about hardship. When we do what is right and appropriate, not by human, but by Divine standard, we are rewarded with goodness, not hardship. This is why we must learn that hardship is a warning for us to correct where we have gone wrong in thought, word, emotion, and deed. And when we correct ourselves by doing what is right, we are blessed with goodness, and hardships cease. This is the infallible Truth concerning all hardship.

Chapter Six

Regression

Man has regressed since the beginning of time. We have been brought low over and over again throughout the ages. However, only very few acknowledge regression, and even fewer recognize it in every generation. Regression is a return to a former or less developed state. It is the opposite of progress and growth.

We must first understand the nature of life before we can understand regression. We were meant to always grow, to always progress, to transform into someone greater than our previous state moment by moment. This is our purpose; this is our cause, and reason for existing. Never should we go retrograde; never should we go back to our former state or a state more backward, but should ever progress and improve in every way, shape, and form.

Never will we find fulfillment if we regress, for our entire existence is wrapped up in growth, progression, and improvement. Regression brings us back to our previous or even lower states of being; to a degraded state based on the progress we have gained over time. Regression strips us of the refinement and resolve we have attained throughout time. Regression brings back the problems that we have solved and overcome, and even brings worse problems. It takes away the very refinement we have and are to embody through experience.

Regression not only takes away our progress, growth and refinement; it does not merely make us stagnant, but it takes away the glory, joy, happiness, satisfaction, and peace of mind we have attained. While we regress we become dissatisfied, oppressed by our current state, and we crave in agony and discontentment to get back to our former stature or even greater.

When we regress we go back to thinking, speaking, feeling and doing the things that caused us pain and struggle. We disregard what we have learned and go back to the ignorance of inexperience and immaturity. We were meant to improve moment by moment with experience. To shed the things and ways that cause us pain, agony, discomfort, and disappointment. We were always meant to grow and become refined through trial, success, and error. To improve in every part of our being and our lives; realizing that we should follow our successes, and avoid the things and ways of error.

If we follow this simple formula we shall never regress. However, man has become so disconnected with the ways of harmony, and the gentle subtlety of conscience, that he follows ignorance in blindness; and so continues to hurt himself in flounder; stripping himself of the light that is ever before him.

Regression only comes when man ignores the subtle guidance that is ever shining on the pathway before him. Without the light one cannot see the guided path, but walks in darkness in hopes of not going astray and getting lost, and even more, to not walk in error and call it wisdom and Truth. Only a few have continued to progress throughout life without regression. And when most regress they never find their way back to the exalted stature of adherence to experience; this is so because it is hard to find your way once you have regressed, unless you place yourself in the position of the light of Truth that is there to elevate you beyond the point of regression.

Regression will always be a problem for those who look back, bringing them back to the previous state that they look upon; stealing progress. This is the infallible Truth regarding all regression.

Chapter Seven

Dishonor

Dishonor is a very important factor in the lives of mankind. It is what averts goodness, Love, and respect. Dishonor is the disharmony of goodness and Love. It is based on selfish and cowardice behavior and attitude above all.

Many live a life of self-centeredness, a trait that diverts the mind from doing the ultimate good, and does things in service to self. This in turn brings pain, discomfort, and hardship. At all times guilt will follow those who choose to do things selfishly. Those who do things only to serve themselves find that they are tormented by the inward and outward state of things because of their actions.

Dishonor is really going out of the way of Love and doing things for selfish reasons that manipulate the mind into thinking that there will be some benefit that comes from it. Focusing on self and not the greater good will always bring heartache and outward circumstances that resist the selfish deed in every way.

The origin of dishonor comes from selfishness, and the only way to divert such dishonor is to be selfless. The very definition of dishonor is selfishness and cowardice. This is so because selfishness serves the wicked end of self, and cowardice serves the wicked end of others because of a lack of courage to do the right thing. Many times the latter is because of opposition, but at every juncture selfishness comes into play because of self-interest with no consideration for the interest of that which is good. Many sometimes feel intimidated by others, which is why they do that which is wrong; but selfishness considers only that of the carnal and mundane, instead of the Divine, the good, and Love. This is dishonor.

Dishonor is defined wholly by selfishness and cowardice simply because it is rooted in either, concerning all circumstances. Both of which will bring torment to the soul until one does what is right. Doing that which does not serve Love and relates goodness is dishonor by definition. When we put ourselves over others we bring disgrace and dishonor upon ourselves, but when we choose to do the good that does not wrong anyone, we honor ourselves as well as everyone else.

The result of dishonor is a long line of inward and outward resistance that will bring pain and hardship until we yield to the honorable thing. It is only when we listen to the voice of conscience and do that which is right will we avert pain and hardship, and as a result start a new cycle of karma; attracting the good and averting the bad.

It is always imperative that we remember that all that does not serve Love, humility, selflessness, self-control, and the ultimate GOOD is by definition, dishonor. And dishonor will always bring resistance of the conscience and the outward state. This happens to push us back to the GOOD we know we have erred against. It is meant to help us to realize and admit that we have done wrong; and to further push us to do what is right; that which will serve the greater good of all. It is only when we give into these signs and portents will we avert resistance and begin a new cycle of karma. There is nothing else that will bring peace of mind. This is so because the conscience speaks out against us when we have done wrong, and will not give us solace until we do what is right; this is the work of Truth to make all things straight by testifying against dishonor. This is the infallible Truth that governs all dishonor in every way, shape, and form.

Chapter Eight

Distraction

Since the very beginning of time, man has been distracted by destructive lusts and desires. As a result he plays the role of his own demise. Whether it is for power, revenge, or vanities, man has been distracted by his own heart. No matter what it is, if it is not for selfless Love and the ultimate good of all, it is a distraction of destruction.

Man can only avert distractions of the heart by ceasing from personal desire; for this is the only escape from the desires that are always seemingly plausible yet are destructive in every way. Mankind must first cease from selfishness, in order not to destroy his inner being. Their every intention must be wrapped up in selflessness. Man must first see that all desire is his own destruction, and as a result turn from the error of his ways.

Only when we realize that nothing good can ever come from selfish desire can we take the first step into the Divine reality and avert every distraction of the heart. That is to step away from all that is associated with self. Man must disassociate himself from self-inspired motives and give himself to selfless service in order to avert the many distractions that come with self-interest. Only then can he start to see the Divine reality that he was created in Love, by Love, to serve Love. This is our whole purpose; there is nothing divine outside of this purpose. And it is only when we give into this reality will we begin to take the path that is laid out before us as created beings.

Think of the HOLY Angels; their entire existence is wrapped up in service, first to GOD and then to man. It is the same approach that we need to take as human beings. Only then can we realize that all the distracting lusts and desires are rendered redundant through selfless service. For the man that takes care of others and puts others and the greater good before self is taken care of by GOD. The Divine reasoning is that the man who puts the greater good before himself at all times need not think of himself. For in putting the greater good before self at all times, the greater good takes care of him because of his selfless nature.

Only when we begin to think in this way will we see all our needs provided for. But the man that always puts himself before all will always find shortage in his needs. However, the man that always puts the greater good before self finds that the greater good provides for him because of his consideration. But when we put selfishness before all things, including the greater good, we find our provisions to always be insufficient. This is because self can in no way, shape, or form provide anything for anyone. However, in serving the greater good we find that the greater good is all sufficient as a provider.

Only when we serve the greater good will we find ourselves void of all selfishness (distractions). Do not serve your wants, but instead serve your need to serve the greater good and you will find that all your distractions that come with consideration towards self is alleviated. It is only then that you will attain Divine focus instead of mundane focus. At this point you will see that all carnality and all that is associated with self is a distraction, void of Divine focus. And in seeing this you will be awakened from your slumber of carnal pursuits.

Serve not your carnal desires, for they are all distractions from the greater good. This is the infallible Truth in regards to distraction.

Chapter Nine

Annoyances

Since the dawn of creation man has endeavored to quell and overcome annoyances. We have failed to realize that the external annoyances of life come from the internal annoyance of imbalance. There is no way to overcome annoyances, except by looking inward and fixing the internal state. This is simply because the external is simply a reflection of the internal state. All that man finds to be annoyances can only be fixed by fixing the inward state through reflection.

Mankind has lost sight of the substantial Truth in the midst of the mundane life; thinking that by making changes in the external environment alone they can bring the bliss that is sought after by everyone. This is at its very core, ignorance and folly. We must first see the external annoyances of life as portents of the internal imbalance that can only be fixed by correcting the internal state. By changing the attitude and disposition of annoyance within we can change the way that all things external affects us, or whether they affect us at all. But first one must acknowledge that the unfortunate external circumstances of life are warnings that the heart needs to be corrected of all its errors. Secondly, we must do some soul searching, looking at the causes of all effects, both internally and externally. And by searching within we can find the problem at hand that causes our external discomfort.

When looking within we must first search out our attitude to the external, and as a result find the internal response that reacts to external stimuli. By searching out the attitude towards the external, we can then look deeper at why we have the attitude that we have of the external. Then when we find the root cause of why react the way we do, we must step back from opinion and take the path of non-resistance. For only by showing no resistance to what annoys will we learn what purpose it serves by stepping away from the push and pull that comes with opinion. At this point the true colors of what annoys and causes discomfort will show its foundation. And by this we can facilitate the inward state that has no discomfort towards external stimuli, or better yet, attract the external condition we need to grow and experience bliss. By allowing the internal condition to flourish without opinion, based on impersonal Love, we will finally be liberated by the Truth to cooperate with the path that causes no discomfort or annoyances whatsoever.

We must learn that never should we push or pull the internal being, but must always give ourselves to the law of impersonal and unconditional Love, and by extension, the push and pull that forms without will become responsive to Truth and Love. Annoyances can only affect us when we choose to be annoyed. But more importantly, we are annoyed when we veer from the Divine path, as a means to bring us on the path of liberation. And by looking at annoyances as an impulse of opinion, or better yet, reproof for error, we can then cooperate and overcome them. It is all a state of mind whether or not we choose to be annoyed, or see annoyances as reproof. It is a choice of the free will whether or not we are annoyed by anything whatsoever, or to cooperate with the Divine direction of all annoyances. And by choosing to not be annoyed by anything, and follow the direction of every annoyance as Divine guidance, we can find bliss. Nothing will ever annoy us unless we allow it to, so we should instead find in every annoyance the Divine will and direction. And by knowing this we are set free with the knowledge of power over every error.

It is best to choose not to be annoyed by anything whatsoever, realizing that all things happen to teach us lessons that we need to learn on the journey of life. By becoming an observer of all that happens without opinion or prejudice, we can harness the lessons that we need to, instead of being annoyed by anything whatsoever. We must will, and choose to think, speak, and do what is right under all circumstances, and by this we will become students as well as teachers of life, and find our annoyances to be direction when in the way of misdirection, instead of becoming agitated. Within all annoyances can be found: the Teacher of life, the Director of Truth, the Enabling of sight, the lighting of the Divine path, the liberation from all error, and the Love of GOD. This is the infallible Truth regarding all annoyances.

Chapter Ten

Form

Form is a particular way in which a thing exists or appears. All forms are hindrances to life. Form is always negative. Form has its substance in selfishness, hatred, jealousy, dishonor, anger, sorrow, distrust, dishonesty, doubt, and irreverence. All these forms take shape in the character and personality. When we choose to give way to opinion and bias we create these forms. Forms make us unsure and unstable. It is form that brings heartache and hardship.

As long as we take form in any way or shape, we are bound to make mistakes. Form makes us insecure, and takes away from us internal and external pleasantness. Only when we take form will we lose ourselves to impulses.

When we think, we must have an opinion of something. And it is thought that makes the decision to lean towards our prejudices. Simply because we have formed opinions of likes and dislikes, we are prone to be bias. Our biases mislead us into thinking our own opinions are Truth. And this is very dangerous since Truth is unbiased and free from opinion. The forming of thoughts and opinions is always out of prejudice and always blinds us from seeing, acknowledging, and knowing the Truth. When we choose to follow our own inclinations we lose sight of the right path. And by losing sight of the right path we fall deeper into our own forms of bias.

Most people have taken on one form or another, losing sight of the Truth in the midst of their own opinions and inclinations. Form goes against the tides of Truth, causing resistance, fault, error, and hardship in our lives. Every form is based on a misconception of the true reality, a misunderstanding of the substantial Truth, a miscalculation of impersonal Love, a misapprehension of the Divine substance, a mistuning of the perfect harmony, and a misjudgment of the correct path. These are the reasons why man has failed miserably to achieve immutable happiness, irrefutable joy, infallible direction, inward perfection, internal fortitude, and immortal transcendence. This is the infallible Truth concerning every form.

Chapter Eleven

Formlessness

Formlessness is having no shape. It is neglect of opinion and personal intellect. Formlessness is the omitting of the personality. It is looking beyond the self for guidance. One can only be formless when all that is personal is neglected, and the personal is replaced by the impersonal. To be formless is to flow with the winds and tides, instead of resisting them. It is giving into what comes our way and dealing with them by not forcing anything, but by adhering to all that seeks us out. Formlessness is an art form, and only comes by the mastery of selflessness. When one forgets the self, then can the formless take the place of selfishness and bias.

One must first neglect the opinions he has and give into the things that come his way as a means of harnessing the lessons he ought to. First one must acknowledge and embrace the fact that all that he encounters serve a purpose in teaching him vital lessons on his life's journey. It is then that he can truly neglect the personal and become a listener of all that he encounters, knowing that he can harness lessons from all things in life. Only then can he rise above the delusions of the bias of the character and personality that he has coveted since his inception; ultimately knowing and cooperating with all that he encounters.

Like a river flowing downstream without any resistance should we be; moving with all that enter our lives in a non-resistant way. It is then that we will be open to see all the lessons we need to harness; unfiltered and unhindered. When we feel resistance in anything whatsoever, it is because we have taken form. And only by taking on ourselves formlessness can we move with the current of destiny without any resistance.

The fact is that all forms will experience resistance and hardship. And only by being formless can we see that nothing really goes against us but ourselves. There is no external enemy, only an internal one. If we will look beyond our wants and desires, and consider that we know nothing of what we need, then we can put our needs before our wants, knowing that our needs are the only necessities for living and improving, and are always supplied without any effort. All that we need always presents itself without our effort. It is just up to us to move in accordance with what is presented to us and cooperate without wanting more.

Our desires will always lead us astray, and only when we are formless, wanting or desiring nothing but to fulfill the will of GOD will we take the first step towards enlightenment. We must desire nothing knowing that all that we need will always be presented to us. And furthermore wanting anything will mislead us into thinking that our desires are more important than our needs, when in fact they are not relevant.

It is up to us to meet everything that comes into our lives with cooperation instead of resistance, for then are we truly wise beyond words. But more than this we should see the things that present themselves in our lives as requirements to teach us the lessons we need to embody. And never should we seek out more than our needs. Wherever we meet resistance we can know that a lesson is being taught, and where we cooperate with the things presented to us we will not find resistance. The key is to not seek out or do more than what is necessary. For our desires will always meet resistance, both within and without. The fact is that we only need to deal with what present themselves to us, instead of going out of our way for our desires. We must let Love lead us, as it is beyond character and personality; it is the true art of formlessness. It is the way to escape from all form; this is the infallible Truth concerning true formlessness.

Chapter Twelve

Ease

Ease comes only after we have achieved formlessness. Many say that life is hard and wish that life could be easy; but they fail to realize that it is within them to live an easy life. They fail to see that they are the ones that cause themselves pain, hardship, and resistance. Most of all they fail to see that desires are their worst enemy, the source of all hardship. This is simply because desires go outside of the realm of necessity. And what is unnecessary will interrupt that which is necessary and form resistance within and without.

The only way to live a life of ease is to turn away from all desires and look towards our destiny. This is always the path of no resistance; the path of no desire. When we let go of desires we find that we are at ease. But when we strive for more than what we need we always find hardship and resistance. All that we need always presents itself; it is only when we deny them and strive for more than what we need will we end up with less, though believing extravagance to be more. Only then will we experience resistance and hardship.

Ease comes to those who acknowledge that they can never care for themselves more than GOD can. And by this acknowledgement wants nothing in life, knowing that all that is needed is already provided before we can even conceive of them. It is only then will we be set free from our wants and desires. Only then will we be liberated from a life of hardship and resistance. All we need to do is to cooperate with the things that present themselves in our lives. And never should we go out of the way of our necessities. Never want more than you need, and never think of your needs, for they are already provided. This is the infallible Truth in regards to ease.

Chapter Thirteen

Attraction

Attraction is the action or power of evoking by thought, emotion, word, and deed. Most people engage attraction without even being aware of it. Many attract the wrong things, and few attract the right things.

One must first have an understanding of how he attracts. We attract first with thought. Every thought attracts the manifestation and nature of the thing that is thought of. Every thought is attached to the internal state of our being. We think about that which relates to our own identity. And we attract what we think. Whether it is good or bad we evoke the things we think about. Every thought, emotion, word, and deed attracts the very essence of what is thought, felt, said, and done. What we think, feel, say, and do internally attracts its essence outwardly.

When we think good thoughts we evoke the good which we think about. The same is applied to the bad. We must learn that evocation/attraction is a simple science. What we think, feel, say, and do will always attract the very essence our thoughts, emotions, words, and deeds, both internally and externally. When we think, feel, say, or do something, we attract that very thing in our lives with exactitude. When we are positive we attract positivity in our lives, and the same can be said about negativity. There is nothing complicated about it. It is just that simple. We are masters of the things we attract in our lives. It begins with a simple thought.

Every thought bears fruit with intricate exactitude; they are the root causes and very nature of all that we experience throughout life. Whatever is manifested externally must first enter the internal mind. Only what we think is ever attracted to us, and nothing that is not first conceived by the inward man can ever be manifested. This is the infallible Truth concerning all attraction.

Chapter Fourteen

Expression

Expression is the action of making known one's thoughts and emotions. Many express themselves in anger, hatred, sorrow, selfishness, and jealousy, simply because these are what they think and feel. However, they do this in ignorance of their purpose. Most people fail to realize that expression is a gift; a gift that should be cherished and held sacred in the heart and mind.

Expression was meant to bring cheer to all; both to the one who expresses and others who experience the expression. It was meant to lift the vibration into Love and positivity. Most people fail to honor this. All expression must be carried on the wings of Love. For this is the sole purpose of our existence. Never should we express ourselves in negativity. We should always express Love in all things, at all times in every way, shape, and form. Otherwise, we will be miserable.

Expression is a tool for fulfillment, and by not using it as such we experience the disappointment and emptiness of all that is good. One must express Love throughout all things and in every moment, not just somethings and sometimes, but in everything and every moment consistently. Love should be our only expression. Every thought, emotion, word, and deed must be unfolded in and with Love.

If we fail to express Love at all times under all circumstances, we will fail to see the light in ourselves and in others. Only when Love encompasses our expression entirely will we truly be free from striving. Love will set us free in every sense of the word on a mental and emotional level. It is then that our souls will be free, and the burden of darkness will be lifted from us utterly. When we express ourselves in Love alone we will have mental clarity, an unburdened conscience, and an unhindered soul.

With Love as our only expression there will be nothing that can cause us to remain stagnant or regress mentally, spiritually, or emotionally. In Love we operate at optimal level with nothing being able to possibly hold us back. Let Love be your guide and master in all expression and you will truly experience peace and bliss like no other. As long as Love is our only expression we will transcend all limitations, and the joy of being will fill our souls. Love is the only expression that can bring infinite value and resolve in and throughout every area of our lives.

Expressing ourselves in Love alone will bring ease like none other, and fulfillment that cannot be achieved by anything else whatsoever. This is the infallible Truth as it concerns expression.

Chapter Fifteen

Divinity

Divinity is not merely the disposition of GOD and angels. It is the state of Holiness. Man also can be Divine by achieving Holiness. However, this cannot be achieved by prayer, but only through sincerity, sacrifice, and much effort. Man must work on his flaws and chip away at them until at last he has become refined and divine. One must search inwardly to the deepest recesses of the heart and mind; of emotion and thought in order to work on improving his disposition until finally at last he finds that there is no flaw in him.

Divinity is a state of being that will only come forth after much struggle to shed the flaws of mortality. One must discard from the heart and mind all that would not express pure Love. And as a result attain the Divinity which he seeks. Only when we let go of all our prejudices and opinions will we take the first step towards achieving

Divinity. We must discard from the mind all pollution and fortify the heart in Holiness in order to achieve Divinity.

When all dross and chaff is discarded from the heart and mind we can then fortify ourselves in Love, which is the identity of Divinity. Divinity can only be achieved by struggle with the carnal and selfish impulse in order let go of all that hinders. All that goes against Love must be rebuked. Otherwise, there is no way to achieve true Divinity. Divinity must be acknowledged and honed as the state of heart and mind that is always conducive of Love. This is the infallible Truth as it concerns all Divinity.

Chapter Sixteen

Selfless

Most people are selfish and live only for themselves. They fail to see the virtue of being selfless. However, there is nothing as fulfilling as a selfless life. Selflessness fulfills all things, including Love. Selflessness gives way to true expression. By being selfless we take the focus off ourselves and direct it towards others, and the ultimate good of all. Selflessness brings true fulfillment and satisfaction. It makes us pleasant within and brings pleasantness without as well.

Selflessness is the way of those who transcend mortality. Realizing that selflessness brings out our true being we are liberated when we live a life of selflessness. For selflessness is not merely random acts of kindness; but is a way of life; a state of being. Selflessness is a life of kindness. When we are selfless we find that all things come together to make us happy. It is only selflessness that conjures the realization that life is not about materialism or carnality, but is about giving all that we can with a selfless heart.

Selflessness is a gift in itself of infinite proportion. From material giving with a loving heart, to kind words, and good deeds, selflessness makes whole both the giver and receiver. It brings the very essence of Love to the forefront. Selflessness sees giving as better than receiving. Those who are selfless at all times in and throughout all things in every way, shape, and form, will never have any problems whatsoever. They will never be concerned about themselves, as selflessness takes care of the selfless. Selflessness will always be the great revealer of Love and Truth. This is the infallible Truth in regards to being selfless.

Chapter Seventeen

Selectivity

Selectivity is the quality of carefully choosing someone or something as the best or most suitable. Most people make decisions from their own biases and desires. However, very few know the art of selectivity. True selectivity can only be honed by selecting all things through the eyes of Love, kindness, and selflessness.

When we choose things out of Love we make the best decisions that we can possibly make. Such selectiveness always goes against our biases. We must learn to choose things because they express Love, and not because it is what we desire. When we do this we live up to our optimal potential. Potential that can only be realized in and through Love.

Let Love encompass all your decisions and you will get the best results that could never be achieved otherwise. Love is the overruling power that brings goodness to those who adhere to it and uses it as a guiding system in and throughout all things, at all times. By using Love as the only guide we find that we always make the best decisions possible. There is no power greater than Love. It governs all things.

When we cooperate with Love we are relieved of every burden. And in using Love as the only guide in making decisions we find freedom and ease like no other. Only when we give into Love above all things will we find true freedom, true expression, and true fulfillment. Love is the only right path to take in all things, and especially in making decisions. This is the infallible Truth as it regards true selectivity.

Chapter Eighteen

Expect Nothing

Most people have expectations based on their desires. Many times only to be disappointed in not seeing the end of what they expect. They fail to realize that never should they expect anything from anything or anyone, but should always let go of expectations. This way they can conquer disappointment in every way, shape, and form. Never to be disappointed by not seeing their expectations brought to fruition.

Mankind expects because of desire. But only when we learn that desires mislead us will we cease from desire. And by not having any desire we cease from expecting anything whatsoever. By not desiring anything we completely eradicate all expectation, and by not expecting anything we confirm that we have no desire.

All that we need for our joy and happiness always presents itself to us; and by not desiring anything and acting on the things that are presented for our wellbeing, we devoid all expectation. We must learn to never expect or desire. For in so doing we will find true fulfillment and satisfaction; true joy and happiness.

Whenever we expect anything we set ourselves up for disappointment. But by not expecting anything there is no possible way for us to be disappointed by anything, no matter what shape or form it is in. Those who expect nothing are free from all burdens; free from all desire. One must exalt the notion to not expect anything at any given time, and thereby be set free from the snare of vanity. In this we are exalted high above the world. This is the infallible Truth as it concerns expecting nothing.

Chapter Nineteen

The Present

Mankind has always given focus to the past and the future; thinking that the past can bring insight and that the future can bring promise. However, the past and the future are irrelevant. We cannot rewind to the past or fast forward to the future. All that we have is the present. And only by living in the present can we solidify the past and the future. The present moment is all that truly count; it is the eternal now that matters. We cannot change the past or be sure of the future. We can only change and be sure of the present.

If we look at the present moment as the only way we can be productive and progress we will find it to be true. The present is when all time and space disappears in the awareness of the moment, not reminiscing of the past or anticipating the future. The present is the only moment we have, the past is just the past and the past and the future is none existent if we live in the moment.

The key to happiness is living and being wrapped up in the present until the shadow of the past and the prospect of the future is lost to the point of none existence in the moment. Those who look at the past and the future would be much better off if they placed their attention on the present moment. You cannot plan to be happy in the past nor in the future, only the present. When we begin to see the present moment as the only moment we will ever have, we can then embrace every moment as the eternal now.

In the rapture of the present all things seem like a miracle, and we begin to see eternity as the moment we live in; life will become one moment for us to always enjoy; one moment to always be happy. In the present we can cease every opportunity, we cannot cease any opportunities in the future, for the future will never be the moment; and the same applies to the past. In the present we can always enjoy ourselves, but not in the future because the future is always yet to come and the past is always gone. For example, if one says that they will do something tomorrow, and when tomorrow comes they do it or not, when tomorrow comes it is the present, not the future nor the past. Therefore, we can only live in the moment, we cannot live in the future nor can we live in the past.

The present is all that we will ever have, not the past, nor the future. Not to say that we are not to plan for the future or learn from the past, but the past can never be reclaimed, neither can we claim the future. When we think of the past or the future we think of them in the present moment. And when we plan for the future and the future comes it becomes the present. Therefore, emphasis should always be placed on the present moment. It is in the present moment that we can make changes, not the past nor the future. So the present is all we have. Living in the present is the secret to living in eternity without discomfort or molestation of the past or future; this is the infallible Truth in regards to the present.

Chapter Twenty

Estimation

Estimation is a rough calculation of the value, quantity, or extent of something. Estimation is necessary all throughout life. Before undertaking anything we should estimate it. By estimating we can make our lives easier. When we estimate we can bring Truth to the forefront, seeing the end of all things before we take part in them.

Estimation goes a long way in securing for us exact timing, and helps us to see ahead of things before they happen. By estimating we can provide exactitude in all things. Only an estimate can make us exact and know when and how to gauge all things. By estimating we know how long to engage anything, and see the limit of all things.

True estimation allows us to take care and to be precise in all that we do. By estimating we can prepare for all things in advance. And through estimation we prevent bad things from happening. Estimations let us place a value and timing on all things. It is sophisticated providence with great simplicity. Those who estimate will find that they are more efficient and effective because of their estimations.

In and throughout all things estimation has its rightful place. In estimations we can find Truth and discernment. In estimation we find resolve and trust. Estimation throughout all things is always helpful. There is nothing that can replace sincere estimation; it is invaluable. Those who estimate all things are truly intelligent as it reveals responsibility. True estimation puts all things into perspective and makes them feasible, as well as reasonable. We should give into the guidance of GOD in order not to under or overestimate anything, anyone, or our own potential. We must first come to GOD as an empty vessel that admittedly knows nothing of its own, but seeks only knowledge and Truth in and throughout all things at every given moment, only then will we achieve exactitude through estimations from the wisdom of GOD. This is the infallible Truth in regards to estimation.

Chapter Twenty One

Power

Power is defined as the ability or capacity to do something or act in a particular way. But power is more than ability; it is the will and authority to do, to influence, and to enforce. One must know that true power comes from within. It comes from inner resolve, knowledge, wisdom, understanding, and ultimately enlightenment. True power comes only from knowing and acting on what we know with tact.

Power is inner strength that is developed from the empowerment of knowing. When we know, we can then assert power. But many misunderstand what power is, they think it means authority over others, and the ability to subdue others into doing their will. However, this could not be further from the Truth. For true power is indeed authority over self. It is subduing the lower passions of self by that which is higher; from the mortal to the immortal; from the perishable to the imperishable; from weakness to strength; from recklessness to control; from the imperfect to the perfect; and from the temporal to the eternal. This is what power is, and it comes only from knowing.

Power is to know and do well; knowing and doing better; and ultimately knowing and doing that which is best. Such knowledge can only come from the internal compass, the still voice within, the conscience. When we learn how to listen to and follow this voice in and throughout all things, then we can have the knowledge of true power. This is the infallible Truth concerning all power.

Chapter Twenty Two

Gratitude

Gratitude is the quality of being thankful; readiness to show appreciation for and to return kindness. Gratitude is a necessary part of life. We must be grateful for all that we have received; all the Truth that we have harnessed; and all the potential that we have.

Gratitude makes life much easier. It is what brings the realization of how blessed we are. We can only be grateful if we let go of all negative thoughts and emotions. It is then that we will truly be conducive of gratitude. When we are in this state, life becomes magical and all things seem good. With gratitude we can put all things into perspective and appreciate life in the very highest.

Gratitude makes all things seem okay, and also help us to accept our current position as a vital one. Gratitude helps us to see beyond the troubles and realize that all things in our lives are plausible. Gratitude is a fruit of maturity that helps us to see all things for what they are. It helps us to accept the role that we need to play. Gratitude never causes discomfort even in the slightest, but brings ease and contentment. Without gratitude life seems hard, as we lose focus of the good and dwell on all that is bad. But with gratitude life becomes easier.

It is gratitude that places focus on all the good things in our lives, forgetting all that besets us, and even helps us to see our besetting as a blessing and warning to show us that we have erred. This is the infallible Truth concerning true gratitude.

Chapter Twenty Three

Direction

Direction is the course along which someone or something moves. Or better yet, the management or guidance of someone or something. Direction is very important in life. It gives us clarity and perspective on life. However, very few understand how to perceive direction. Many have ideas and thoughts that mislead them. They fail to realize that Love, kindness, humility, selflessness, and the path of least resistance can bring true direction.

In and throughout all things these are immutable in giving perspective and taking away the delusions that we conceive. Self-consideration can in no way, shape, or form give direction. We must give into the immutable law of Love in order to be directed on the right path at all times. Without Love as our guide we are lost. We must first look beyond all self-interest and look to Love in order to be led aright.

In every sphere of life, only Love can give direction with impeccable exactitude. We must learn the art of Love in order to direct and be directed in the right way. We need to look to our internal guiding system in order to know how, when, why, as well as the proportion in which to administer Love. Without listening to that still voice of discernment we will be lost. Not knowing the specifics of administering Love.

When we give ourselves to discerned Love, we can then be directed with artful precision. Love is never wrong and will never mislead us as long as we use it with adherence to the inner voice of discernment. This is the infallible Truth in regards to direction.

Chapter Twenty Four

Trust

Trust is the firm belief in the reliability, integrity, or ability of someone or something. Knowing the definition of trust we should also know that Love is the only reliable source that we can depend on at all times. Love is the integrity of Truth, and only Truth can be the true foundation of trust. Without Love and Truth we are misled. Therefore, it is essential that we give ourselves to Love as the only thing we trust.

When we trust Love we trust the all-powerful essence that will reveal all truth. And by the revelation of truth we are led aright. We cannot trust in self-interest and self-consideration without being misled. Nor can we trust in hate or biases without being deceived. Only Truth is worthy of trust, and Love brings us all Truth. And Truth will always be what we need in order to flourish and prosper in and throughout all things in every way, shape, and form.

Truth is the integrity of trust, and Love is the integrity of Truth. This is the order and the nature of all things true. Trust in Love as well as the internal compass that facilitates Love and you will never be deceived, ever knowing the trust of infallible Truth.

Trust is necessary in order for us to proceed in and throughout all things at all times. Without trusting in something or someone we will not entertain the idea of following them. Trust will always be liberated by Love and Truth; and this is why they are needed in all things in order to proceed throughout life. Without trust we will not feel comfortable with anything or anyone whatsoever. Love and Truth gives the assurance we need to know that something is safe and favorable so we may trust in them. This is the infallible Truth concerning all trust.

Chapter Twenty Five

Enlightenment

Enlightenment is a final spiritual state marked by the absence of desire or suffering. Enlightenment is the highest state of consciousness. It is higher than knowledge, wisdom, and understanding. It is the consciousness that is above desire, and by extension suffering. For without desire there can be no suffering. Desires are the source of all suffering. When we desire something and do not manifest it, it then brings suffering. Only when we let go of all desire can we truly enter the state of enlightenment.

Enlightenment is higher awareness above all that causes suffering. When we let go of every desire we then see that all our needs are provided for in the state of being desire-less. By being aware of the fact that desire only causes suffering and has no virtue we enter the heightened state of enlightenment.

Only when we become aware of Truth can we enter the state of enlightenment. For the awareness of Truth brings resolve and closure in all things. If we harness the Truth then we will harness enlightenment. For Truth and enlightenment is one in the same. Truth sets us free and sets us on the right path without hindrances; making the way clear for us to live up to our potential at optimum level. Enlightenment enables us to shake off the delusion of falsehood and live in the light of Truth.

It is only when we look beyond our prejudices and desires and look towards the path of least resistance in and throughout all things in every way, shape, and form will we embody enlightenment. And by this we will be free from the molestation of desires and prejudices that resist the path of Truth. This is the infallible Truth in regards to true enlightenment.

Chapter Twenty Six

Sustenance

Sustenance is something that maintains and preserves someone or something in life or existence. When people think of sustenance they think of food and drink. However, true sustenance goes way beyond the physical aspect of maintenance. True sustenance is aligning ourselves with Truth and taking the path that is laid out before us. Sustenance exists first on the mental level, then the emotional level, and then the spiritual level.

Mental sustenance has to do with clarity; clarity that can only be found when listening to the still voice of Truth and reproof within. Emotional sustenance has to do with emotional stability; not having discomfort or instability of feelings. Emotional stability can only be attained when we follow our hearts; those things that make us happy. When we veer away from the things that make us happy we feel discomfort and emotional instability. Therefore, we must listen to the things that speak to our joy, happiness, and wellbeing. Spiritual sustenance has to do with spiritual stimuli; that which speaks to our overall sense of Truth and direction. When we follow this path we then become at ease, instead of feeling out of place as if something is missing; like there is a hole that needs to be filled.

The combination of the mental, emotional, and spiritual sustenance provides all the stability we need, and goes infinitely further than desires. For when we desire we focus on what we want instead of what we need. And our wants replaces stability with instability. Therefore, if the mental, emotional, and spiritual sustenance is in place we need never to think of physical sustenance. For the mental, emotional, and spiritual plane provides sustenance for the physical plane in every, way, shape, and form. When the mental, emotional, and spiritual planes are in order, then will the physical sustenance fall under their provisions. As a matter of fact, those who set the mental, emotional, and spiritual plane in order will liberate physical hunger for as long as they align these three planes of being with enlightenment. This has been proven by some in the Far East, and even by the story of Moses on Mount Sinai, but to the western world of desire, lust, and delusion, it is impossible.

The only source of true sustenance on every plane of our existence is Love, selflessness, and nirvana (desire-less-ness). Only those who separate themselves from the carnal and from all desire will experience true sustenance. The sustenance of mental clarity, of emotional stability, and of spiritual fulfillment, is the only true sustenance. This is Divine sustenance; sustenance of the transcendent. This is the infallible Truth concerning all sustenance.

Chapter Twenty Seven

Sacrality

Sacrality means to make sacred. Very few understand the meaning of sacred, and even fewer try to make anything sacred. Sacredness is reverence towards something or someone.

We must first understand that all things are to be sacred to us. From human life, animal life and even plant life, we should consider all things sacred. Even what, how, why, where, and when we eat should be considered as sacred. Eating itself should become a sacred act. Sleeping, speaking, thinking, and doing at all times should be held as sacred. Every aspect of our being should be upheld as sacred, even our feelings. We can only validate sacredness in our lives when we look at and hold all things as sacred and put aside all things for Holy use. In doing so we will ourselves become Holy.

Every aspect and activity of our lives should be considered and dealt with as sacred. We should always look beyond the veil of the carnal and mundane and see all things as an opportunity to honor GOD. We can only do this by consecrating all things in our lives as worship, even the most seemingly trivial of things such as when we go to sleep, when we eat and drink, and the way we speak. We should ask the INFINITE ONE for guidance in all things to always think, say, do, and feel all things to HIS GLORY. Otherwise, nothing in our lives will be sacred, but will become mundane and impulsive; irrational and irrelevant.

In order for us to truly become at one with sacredness, all things must become sacred unto us to the GLORY of GOD. This is the infallible Truth as it concerns sacrality.

Chapter Twenty Eight

Dedication

Dedication is the quality of being dedicated or committed to a task or purpose. Dedication is a necessary part of life in and throughout all things, at all times. We must know that without dedication we cannot accomplish anything whatsoever.

One must first of all be dedicated to goodness, to Love, to kindness, to selflessness, to the desire-less state. In so doing he will become refined. He will know the Truth if he dedicates himself to Holiness. And by knowing Truth he will be set free without the hindrances that come with desire, ignorance, and delusion. In and throughout all things at all times we must dedicate ourselves to do only that which is necessary, nothing more and nothing less. If we should dedicate ourselves, not just to learning, but to applying what we have learned, then learning will truly serve its purpose. Experience is a teacher, but should do more for us than just teach us lessons, but instead make us at one with Truth through correct application. Making known that all things are connected, and that dedication to learning and applying what we have learned is the means by which we reconcile all things for our edification and ease of life.

Learning is being aware with the obligation to become one with the awareness, and many times bring delusion instead of Truth when we do not act according to what we have learned. However, experience is being at one with all things. It is in this Truth that dedication is liberated. For only when we dedicate ourselves to experience do we become at one with what we experience, instead of merely becoming aware.

The point is that dedication is being at one with experience, being wrapped up with the experience with die-hearted loyalty and becoming its integrity.

Everything is an experience, and by dedicating ourselves to the experience we become at one with it. It is the experience of dedication and dedication to experience that will truly exalt dedication in and throughout all things as the integrity of accomplishment, knowledge and true wisdom. This is the infallible Truth as it regards dedication.

Chapter Twenty Nine

Identity

Identity is the fact of being who or what a person or thing is. Many are quick to define themselves in many ways. Some will say that they are cheerful, funny, kind, loving, selfless, passionate, creative, subtle, gentle, hopeful, faithful, protective, defensive, and the list goes on. However, anyone who chooses to define himself through his own eyes speaks only half truths, and does not look at himself through the eyes of the unbiased.

We must first understand that we are not separate from anything good or bad unless we develop thoughts and ways of goodness or defilement. And we cannot be pure and defiled at the same time. We must be one or the other. Whether it is suffering or relief, hardship or ease, hate or Love, selfishness or kindness, ignorance or wisdom; most have a little bit of each of these traits within themselves unless they give their efforts to singularize their purpose, lives and ways. Only a few have attained the Holy state and have released unholy ways and habits from their entire existence, but most have much negativity which they consider to be positive, and darkness which they consider to be light.

Most have the same identity at different frequencies. Some are bad, some are worse, and others are the worst. Just as some are good, some are better, and others are the best. Some are caring while others are hateful, some are wise while others are ignorant, and some are Holy while others are unholy. We cannot be two things at the same time. However, some are holier than others, while some are more impure than others, but we all have the same traits, just in different proportions.

We all have the identity, either of light or darkness; some have more light than others, and some have more darkness than others. But we all do have the same identity in goodness or evil, positivity or negativity. However, there are always a select few in every generation that live lives of extraordinary Holiness and some of extreme wickedness. It is by our ways, our lives, our hearts and our mental states that we are defined in either purity or defilement, but there are many frequencies and levels of proportion between the two. This is the infallible Truth in regards to identity.

Chapter Thirty

Necessity

Necessity is the state or fact of being required. Many have a misconception of necessity. They think that all they need is shelter, food, and clothing. More than all, what we need is peace of mind, emotional stability, and spiritual fulfillment. Once these things are in place all other things will seem to be trivial and unnecessary.

We need peace of mind because without it we are confused. We need emotional stability because without it we are unstable in every sense of the word. We also need spiritual fulfillment because without it our souls are tormented. Peace of mind only comes when we align ourselves with the Truth that we need at the specific stage of our lives that we have reached. Emotional stability only comes when we let go of the things we cannot control and accept our current position as it is.

And spiritual fulfillment comes only when we lean towards knowledge, wisdom, understanding, and enlightenment.

Unless we align ourselves with the Truth necessary to our current position in life we will be like wanderers searching for pleasantness and satisfaction in external things. We must know and embrace the Truth in every sphere of our being. For only then will we be contented, uplifted, and trusting of the light that will set us free.

Only mental, emotional, and spiritual pleasantness is ever necessary. Anything else is a want and desire that we can survive without. Better yet, we will always be better off with just our necessities and neglecting our wants and desires. This is the infallible Truth concerning all necessity.

Chapter Thirty One

Perfection

Perfection is the state of being correct and complete in every way. Very few believe that perfection is attainable by human beings in any way, shape, or form. But even fewer have and will ever attain it. We must first let go of the notion that perfection is unattainable. For in fact Christ said **'be ye therefore perfect, even as your FATHER which is in Heaven is perfect.' Matthew (5:48).** In knowing that it is possible to be perfect we become attuned to feeling the need to be perfect. Therefore, we must look at what it takes to be perfect.

First of all perfection has to be based on goodness. For in goodness is the integrity of perfection. Morals and ethics must be first priority for those who wish to attain perfection. And the only way in which we can validate morality and ethics is through Love. Pure and unconditional Love will always pave the way for all goodness. When we put Love above and before us in and throughout all things, at all times, in every way, shape, and form, then we will know perfection.

Perfection should be the ultimate goal of everyone in order to embody true refinement. For without refinement we are flawed, vulnerable, and immature. However, perfection brings resolve and closure with a sense of control and maturity in all things on every point. When we put Love as the only thing before and above us to guide us in and throughout all things at all times, we will never be left at fault. Love will make us blameless and true. In fact, it is Love that will make all things new. It is what will replenish the soul and edify the mind flawlessly. Love is what will set the heart free and give us true selfless expression.

Love will make us kind and bring us fulfillment in every way, shape, and form. Without Love there is no guidance, no Truth, no honor, no justice, and no mercy. Love is the integrity of life itself. Love is the source of all light, without it we are blind. In the integrity of Love we will find true perfection. This is the infallible Truth as it concerns perfection.

Chapter Thirty Two

The Infallible Truth

Infallible means incapable of making mistakes or being wrong. Truth is the quality or state of being true. These two are one in the same. Infallibility is Truth, and Truth is infallibility. Truth is never wrong, but is always right. We can only be conducive of infallible Truth when we let go of all our opinions and prejudices. Only then will we embrace and promote Truth in the very highest.

Many of us stifle our internal compass that guides us in and throughout all things; the voice that goes against our biases. It is that voice that says yes when something is right and no when something is wrong. It is the voice of acceptance and assurance, of correction and reproof. We need to strengthen the voice of conscience through adherence.

Follow the inner voice, as it is the voice of infallible Truth and Love, and you will never go wrong. Love is the integrity and fullness of Truth, and Love and Truth has no limitations or hindrances. They are also one in the same. Love and Truth are interchangeable similitudes. The realm of thought can either be confirmed or rejected by them with infallible precision. This is why we need to think with the voice of conscience without fear. It is quite simple, if it feels good to think a thought then conscience approves, if not then it disapproves, the same is applied with deeds. This is infallible Truth.

When I do good, I feel good. When I do bad, I feel bad. That's my religion. – Abraham Lincoln

The infallible Truth is that we are not finite creatures, but are infinite in value and potential. It is only left for us to harness our limitless potential to become one with infinity. And only by thought can we do this. Our thoughts place value on us based on our own perspective of ourselves and all things. The Truth is whatever we believe; whatever we believe to be true becomes our reality, though it might not be the Divine reality. Therefore, if we believe that we are finite and temporal beings then we become finite and temporal. But if we think that we are unlimited and eternal beings, then we become unlimited and eternal. It all begins with thought.

The sum of our entire existence begins and ends with our own thoughts. Therefore, if we think in finite terms we take on the form of such thoughts. Whatever forms our thoughts take on, we ultimately become them. All sickness and health, all poverty and wealth, all deception and Truth, all lack and abundance, all hate and Love, begins in the realm of thought. We choose what, how, why, when, and where to think. We empower and weaken ourselves by our own thoughts. The only choice we ever have is over our own thoughts.

The way we think affects the effects that all things have on us based on the root thought. All thoughts are causes, and we can choose to develop the realm of thought within ourselves from the inner being without external stimuli. However, the majority of people who has ever lived developed thoughts from the external, instead of the internal cause. However, every external thing that evokes our thoughts is connected to internal concepts that we form around the external.

We can form our own thoughts from the internal being, or we can be influenced of what to think based on the external through concepts formed around them. These are the only ways in which we can formulate thoughts. However, most people only think of what to think, and not how to think, and many times what they think is error. Only a very few who has ever lived knows how to think.

There are only two poles of thought; these are the positive and negative poles. All thought has its integrity in either the negative or positive pole. We are just left with whether we will use the two poles in our thinking, or if we will only ever lean to one pole throughout all our thoughts. By this we can formulate all thoughts by either one or both sides of the pole. The value of our thoughts will determine our worth. This is the infallible Truth; truly immutable.

Poem- The Infallible Truth

To set the mind free beyond belief; bringing selfishness to its knees; and bringing forth relief. Liberating Truth; and making carnality mute. Relinquishing ego, in order to bring forth the vision of more, so we can soar. And eliminating sorrow; for a better tomorrow. Knowing no hardship; and giving pardon.

Transcending regression; in order to further the mission. And diminishing dishonor; until all that is left is honor. Paying no attention to distractions; to bring forth the answers. Remembering no annoyances; to the point of peace and flawlessness. Vanquishing all form into formlessness.

Bringing ease and appease. Bringing attraction; to formless mansions. Bringing all expression; to divine repression. Taking Divinity; into infinity. Making selfless; the restless. Making decisions with selectivity; supplying Holy electricity. Expecting nothing; but giving immense loving.

Living life in the present; without relent. Living the estimation; of the sacred station. Endowing with power; the kind Lover.

Forging the attitude of gratitude. Bringing direction in every selection. Shaking the dust off trust. Opening up the mind with enlightenment that supplies strength. Harnessing the only sustenance; to make us stand.

Defining sacrality, above all prideful vanity. Teaching how to dedicate; and embody life experiences to relate. Revealing the true identity, of every entity; doing all things out of necessity. Endowing perfection, through reflection; awakening the mind to inception. Above me and you; is the infallible Truth; that truly cannot be mute.

The End

MIX
Papier aus verantwortungsvollen Quellen
Paper from responsible sources
FSC® C105338

Printed by Books on Demand GmbH, Norderstedt / Germany